PALOMA BLANCA

Illustrated by **PAULA KRANZ**

WHAT IF I FEEL...

AFRAID

W. Books

Dados Internacionais de Catalogação na Publicação (CIP) de acordo com ISBD

B236w   Barbieri, Paloma Blanca Alves

       What if I feel... afraid / Paloma Blanca Alves Barbieri ; traduzido por Karina Barbosa dos Santos ; ilustrado por Paula Kranz. – Jandira : W. Books, 2025.

       32 p. ; 24cm x 24cm. – (What if I feel...)

       Tradução de: E se eu sentir... medo
       ISBN: 978-65-5294-226-5

       1. Literatura Infantil. 2. Emoções. 3. Sentimentos. 4. Medo. 5. Psicologia. 6. Saúde. 7. Saúde mental. I. Santos, Karina Barbosa dos. II. Kranz, Paula. III. Título. IV. Série.

                                          CDD 028.5
2025-1831   CDU 82-93

Elaborada por Vagner Rodolfo da Silva - CRB-8/9410

Índice para catálogo sistemático:
1.   Literatura infantil 028.5
2.   Literatura infantil 82-93

This book was printed in Melon Slices and Metallophile font.

This is a W. Books publication, a division of Grupo Ciranda Cultural.
© 2025 Ciranda Cultural Editora e Distribuidora Ltda.
Publisher: Elisângela da Silva
Text © Paloma Blanca A. Barbieri
Illustrations © Paula Kranz
Translation: Karina Barbosa dos Santos
Proofreading: Adriane Gozzo
Design: Fernando Nunes / Cover: Natalia Renzzo

First published in June 2025
www.cirandacultural.com.br

"Emotions are the colors of the soul; they are spectacular and incredible. When you don't feel, the world becomes dull and colorless."
William P. Young

I dedicate this book to my gigantic family (especially my mother, Creusa), who has given me and continues to give the most beautiful and diverse emotions!

Some situations make me feel a little scared...
and sometimes even terrified.

Like when night falls, and the whole house gets dark.

8

My heart pounds in my chest.

THUMP-THUMP!

THUMP-THUMP!

CLICK!

10

Then, I turn on the light, gather my courage, and say, "Go away, Mr. Fear!"

When my friends invite me to take on a big challenge, I get goosebumps all over.

Whenever a storm comes with loud thunder and bright lightning, I get so scared that I start to shake.

But when Mommy and Daddy hold me tight, I know everything will be okay, and there's nothing to fear.

Some animals really frighten me. I'm scared of snakes, spiders, frogs... and even cockroaches!

Whenever my parents walk away from me, I feel completely lost.

But when they explain where they're going and when they'll be back, little by little, my fear fades away.

When I make new friends, I feel a huge fear of losing them.

In those moments, Mommy always says something that comforts me: "Some friends come and go, dear. What matters is keeping them forever in your heart".

I'm also really scared of trying something new and different.

But I know that feeling this way is normal.
After all, it happens to everyone!

BEAR

24

Some nights, I wake up frightened by nightmares of ghosts and strange creatures.

Whenever that happens, Mommy and Daddy tell me there's nothing to be afraid of, because not everything is what it seems.

Feeling afraid isn't very fun, but many times, fear helps protect me from real dangers.

Other fears, though, I face with great courage!

How do you feel today?

Thankful

Sad

Happy

Angry

Afraid

Loving

Take a little moment to talk about how you're feeling right now.

Talking About Fear

To learn how to deal with fear, we first need to understand what caused it. It's important to think about and talk about this feeling so we can let it go. Read the questions below and reflect on each one:

- What makes you feel scared?
- How do you feel or react when you're afraid?
- When was the last time you felt scared?
- How did you handle that feeling?

Some fears are important because they protect us from danger. Others, though, if we don't face them, can prevent us from experiencing amazing moments and big adventures.

To overcome fear, we need to approach it with confidence. Remembering how strong and brave we are can help push fear away. So, whenever you feel afraid, think about your inner strength and repeat these affirmations:

- I am safe!
- I am as brave as a superhero!
- I can face my fears!
- As I take deep breaths, my fear fades away!

Children, Animals, and Feelings

Children are usually fascinated by pets, and it's no wonder why! Besides being loving and great friends, pets bring joy to a home, improve our health, and create a wonderful sense of well-being.

Having a pet (whether it's a kitten, a puppy, or a bunny) can teach children important values like patience, respect, kindness, affection, and responsibility.

Also, when they're with animals, children find the confidence and self-esteem they need to solve their problems and even deal with their own feelings.

A Message for the Family

The discovery of emotions can be a surprising and challenging moment for children, especially when those emotions are difficult to handle. That's why this book aims to show little ones how and when the feeling of fear appears and how important it is to experience it in all moments.

During this process of exploring emotions, families and educators are invited to see fear from a different perspective: the child's! After all, children have a unique and special way of seeing everything that happens around them.

Dealing with certain emotions is not easy, whether for adults or children. That's why the earlier little ones understand their emotions, the sooner they will develop autonomy and confidence—essential skills for navigating this incredible journey we all share: life!

PALOMA BLANCA was born in a coastal city in São Paulo. Passionate about languages, she pursued a degree in literature and specialized in translation and teaching.

She has loved writing since childhood; in her stories and poems, she would express everything she felt, as writing became the perfect way for her to explore and understand her emotions. Writing this book has been a true gift, one she hopes to share with families, especially with children who, just like she did in her childhood, wish to learn how to navigate the whirlwind of emotions that arise throughout life.

PAULA KRANZ is the mother of two wonderful girls. When she became a mother, her heart was flooded with countless emotions. She embraced the opportunity to transform all the fear, sadness, anger, and immense joy she experienced into feelings that helped her grow as a person.

Together with her daughters, she reconnected with the magical world of childhood. In recent years, alongside playing pretend, building sandcastles, and doodling, she has also specialized in children's books, illustrating many published works. She is filled with dreams and an eagerness to capture the delicacy and lightness of childhood, bringing to life the magic, the sparkle in children's eyes, and their unique way of seeing the world—something they share with us every single day.